FAME

Also by Brad Benedict: **Phonographics**

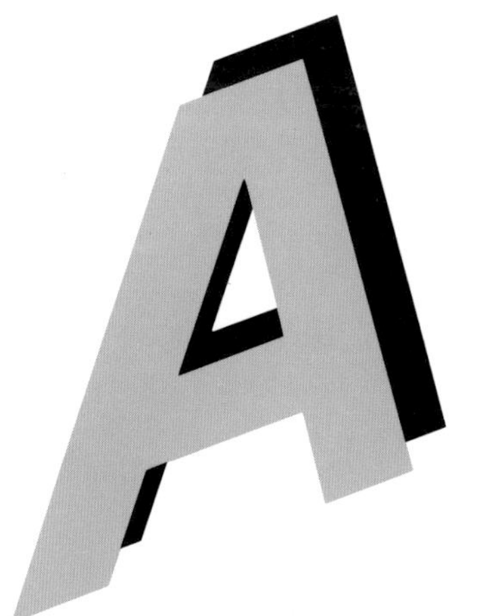

Brad Benedict

H

Harmony Books/New York

To all the exceptional artists and designers whose support and cooperation have enabled me to share their special talents.

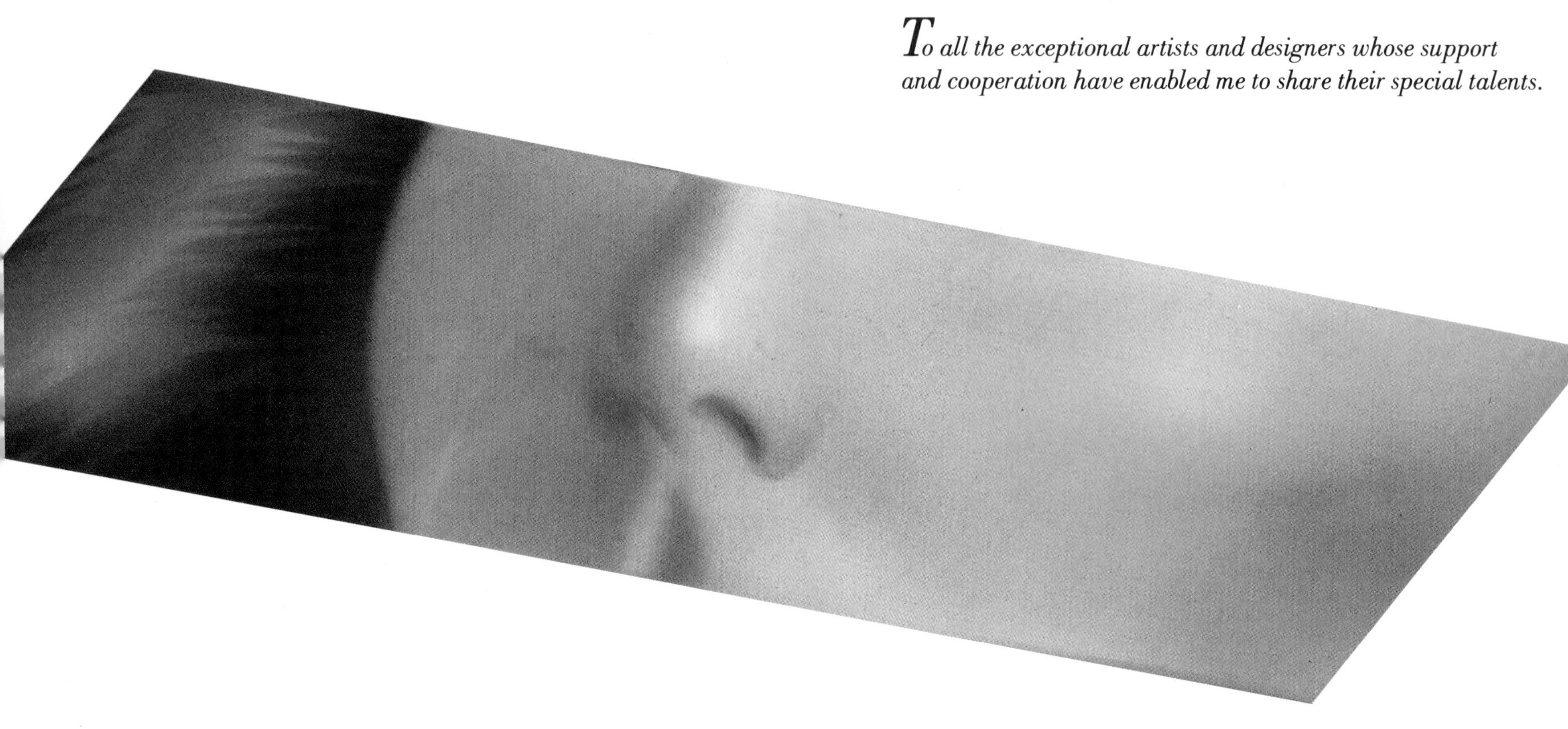

Inquiries should be addressed to Harmony Books, a division of Crown Publishers, Inc., One Park Avenue, New York, New York 10016

Cover Art: Richard Bernstein

Design: Michael Fink

Printed in Japan
Published simultaneously in Canada
by General Publishing Company Limited

Library of Congress Catalog Card Number 80-14440

ISBN: 0-517-541610 (cloth)
ISBN: 0-517-541629 (paper)

10 9 8 7 6 5 4 3 2 1
First Edition

PREFACE

The idea for Fame grew out of my last book, Phonographics, the art of record album covers. I wanted my new book to reflect the changes and accomplishments of recent illustration. The more I looked, the more I discovered: illustration had moved from album covers and posters into the mainstream of commercial art. The work represented here now appears on editorial pages and magazine covers, in advertising, and on pop products like cards and buttons. It has become a familiar part of the visual landscape—so familiar, in fact, that much of the art goes unnoticed and, so, unappreciated. By presenting this work in a book format, where it can stand on its own, apart from the products it was created to enhance, it takes on new meaning. The illustrator's talents can be fully appreciated and contrasted.

The movement of illustration into the mass media is partially a result of our fascination with personalities, recognizable celebrities, and newsmakers. The cult of the personality, around which revolves so much commercial effort—from books to movies to shaving cream—has created a wealth of art, wonder, and vision. Like Vargas with his pin-ups, current illustrators have extended our imagination. Their portraits and caricatures capture the fun, fascination, and irony of the famous.

Fame is a collection of both commercial and personal statements. As I mentioned, some of the work has already appeared. For example, The Who (Gary Panter 1979) was a piece commissioned by Time, and Ronald Reagan (Robert Grossman 1967) was an editorial illustration in Cavalier. But much of Fame has not been seen outside art circles. There is portfolio work, like Barbra Streisand (Richard Amsel 1972) and Paul McCartney (David Edward Byrd 1975), and pieces created especially for the book, like James Garner (Cynthia Marsh 1980) and Woody Allen (Kathy Staico Schorr 1980). The selection of celebrities in Fame is somewhat happenstance: I went first to the artists for their favorites and only later requested that they add a few personalities to round out the book. The famous are their famous as well as my own.

On the pages that follow are the works of many of the best current illustrators. They come from all parts of the world and are joined by a commercial sensibility and a uniqueness of vision. Fame opens with Liz 1963 and Marilyn 1964 by Andy Warhol. He is, in many ways, the inspiration behind this book, and his work sets much of its tone. Fame has many artistic styles, but the use of the airbrush—with its unique ability to give a smooth transition tone and clean sharp edges—stands out. In the work of Peter Palombi (Castro 1975), Todd Schorr (Flash Gordon 1980), Charles White III (Einstein 1973), Kim Whitesides (Dylan 1974), and David Willardson (Linda Ronstadt 1977), the force and beauty of the airbrush comes across.

There are various other distinct styles in Fame: the use of watercolors by Philip Hays (Jim Jones 1979) and Tim Lewis (Pavarotti 1980), and the collage/mixed media approach by Lou Beach (King Tut 1978) and Jim Heimann ("Little Shirley" 1977) form an interesting contrast. A photo-based style like Richard Bernstein's (Liza Minnelli 1979) is able to present the glamour of fame. Artists in this mode, like Paul Jasmin (Marisa Berenson 1979), Ron Lieberman (Lily Tomlin 1977), and Lisa Powers/Taki Ono (Esther Williams 1979), usually work over a photograph or stat and create their pieces with poster paints, dyes, cut paper, and careful brushwork. The influence of fashion strengthens their style.

Pencils and pastels are used by artists like Antonio (Diana Ross 1972), David Croland (Catherine Deneuve 1979), Patricia Dryden (Sylvia Syms 1978), and William Shirley (Marlon Brando 1974). There is beauty and drama in these portraits. Traditional oils and acrylics on canvas are the painterly base of works by David McMacken (Frank Zappa 1972), Neon Park (Marilyn Duck 1978), and Philip Slagter (Elizabeth II Anticipating Bloomingdale's 1977). This is only a sample of the styles and techniques in Fame; each of the artists has a personal attitude that is conveyed in his art, and you must look to see it.

The point of this book, like that of fame itself, is recognition. These portraits and caricatures bring their subjects alive, whether they provoke fun or express admiration. I hope Fame will be enjoyed.

—Brad Benedict

FAME IS MAGIC

Reagan is a mouse. Monroe never looked better than at 50. Lily Tomlin hitches a ride, and Woody Allen is all taped up. Catherine Deneuve is waiting to hold you, while Kissinger is arrested and Jayne Mansfield vamps as a duck. But, best of all, there is magic in Santa's smile. He's made it. He's famous now too.

We are all attracted to fame. The famous are talked about, watched, and dreamed of—we cheer for them, put their pictures on our walls, and discuss their success or misfortune. As you look through Fame, notice the number of celebrities you recognize and consider how much you know about them. Like magic, these personalities have risen above the rest of us; with a little glitter and luck, they have made a place in the daily world. We share our lives with them.

Famous faces are everywhere. They appear on magazine covers, posters, cards, and buttons. It's almost as if by watching or wearing these faces we expect the fame to rub off. But what we are really wearing are dreams. The famous become symbols, shared myths of success: they have made it and their lives are somehow better than ours. A button or a magazine article is a license to dream, to imagine we are part of their world. The more we dream, the more we are released from the ordinariness of our lives. By imagining the famous, we get out of ourselves and extend the boundaries of what we think we can be. It's no surprise famous faces are everywhere.

Fame creates heroes. Personalities become objects of awe and assume power over us. They sell products and advocate causes. They can stand in defiance or quietly lead us to accept the status quo. The art in this book does wonders: it forces us to step back and see in a new way. Look at Larry Flynt as a nun, Jerry Ford eating ice cream, or Ralph Nader disguised as the Lone Ranger. Through the art of caricature, illustrators like Heiner, Punchatz, Willardson, and others put a healthy smile on our faces and remind us how human these people really are. We may not be so easily persuaded or awed next time around.

The famous take on a sense of authority and achievement. They are examples set before us, on T-shirts and TV. But with achievement comes the responsibility of accomplishing more, of giving more. Our demands must deeply annoy them. The careers of stars like Elvis Presley, Marilyn Monroe, and Janis Joplin show that the famous are not always up to the calling. It's the least we can do to give them a second life in our lives.

Fame is capricious, yet sometimes success is well deserved. The portraits of Golda Meir, Bruce Springsteen, and Henry Fonda (among others) remind us that there are still people with special gifts and private talents beyond our reach. We are glad to be in the world with them. Their fame enriches us all.

One of the many sides to fame is the frivolous. Personalities are built up in a flash and gain a following. They humor us. We wonder how they got where they are. Here are illustrations of Spock, Farrah Fawcett, Kiss, and Billy Carter. All you do is add the hype.

Fame has a dark side as well. It rewards with attention the Idi Amins and G. Gordon Liddys of the world. Perhaps it's better that these people are famous, where they can remain in the public eye. We know what they can do behind our backs.

And who could forget the celebrities who are famous only for being famous? Do they deserve more than the fifteen minutes of fame Warhol has assigned to their future? Or the length of time it takes to unbraid your Bo Derek corn rows? Like mirrors in a fun house, these personalities create illusions of grandeur and really have very little substance. "10" today, gone tomorrow.

The artists in Fame succeed in renewing the legends of great stars. As we look at Groucho in a bathing suit with that infectious smile, images from all his old movies come bouncing back in our minds. As the legends of the past are renewed through the nostalgia of the present, the future becomes brighter. Our favorite stars will always be with us. Turn on A Night at the Opera. Let's laugh and dream.

Fame is really about the best of current illustration. Like a good song or poem, a strong illustration focuses experience and allows us to see more in what may appear at first to be very little. These artists capture our imaginations and present the fashion, glamour, and hope of success that attracts us all to fame.

Some last words: the real test of fame is time. Whom will we still recognize in five years? I've written down my guesses—have you? It seems odd to see Phil Ochs, John Travolta, Vincent Van Gogh, and Phyllis Diller in the same book. But diversity is the fun of Fame.

—Peter H. Shriver

In the future everybody will be famous for fifteen minutes.
–Andy Warhol

Liz *Andy Warhol 1963*

Marilyn *Andy Warhol 1964*

Faye Dunaway and Bela Lugosi *Robert Giusti 1974*

Woody Allen *Peter Palombi 1976*

Lovely Rita *Carol Bouman 1980*

Dietrich *Todd Curtis 1980*

Young Clark Gable *Victor Stabin 1977*

Cary Grant *Robert Grossman 1971*

Julie Christie and Warren Beatty *William Shirley 1978*

Liz and Dick *Charles E. White III 1970*

Paul McCartney *David Edward Byrd 1975*

KISS *Michael Doret 1976*

Eddie Money *Cynthia Marsh 1978*

Ike and Tina Turner *Doug Johnson 1973*

Bruce Springsteen *Don Weller 1974*

Dustin Hoffman *Richard Milholland 1979*

Paul Newman *Nick Taggart 1978*

Marlon Brando *Dennis Mukai 1979*

Richard Gere *Richard Bernstein 1979*

James Dean
Pater Sato 1976

Peggy Lee *David McMacken 1976*

Dolly Parton *Linda Stokes 1979*

Dionne Warwick *Don Weller 1970*

Diana Ross *Robert Risko 1976*

Barbra Streisand *Richard Amsel 1972*

Sylvia Syms *Patricia Dryden 1978*

Maria Muldaur *John Lykes 1978*

Werner Erhard *Lou Beach 1977*

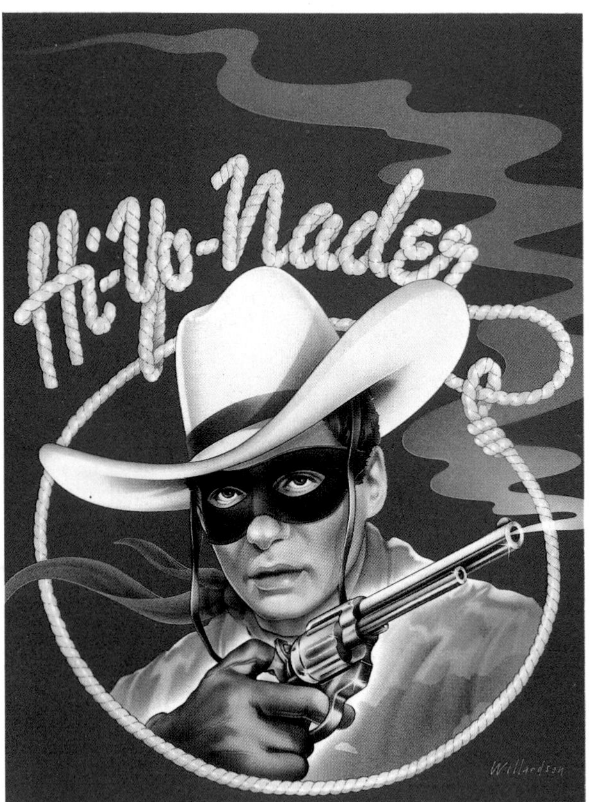

Ralph Nader *David Willardson 1974*

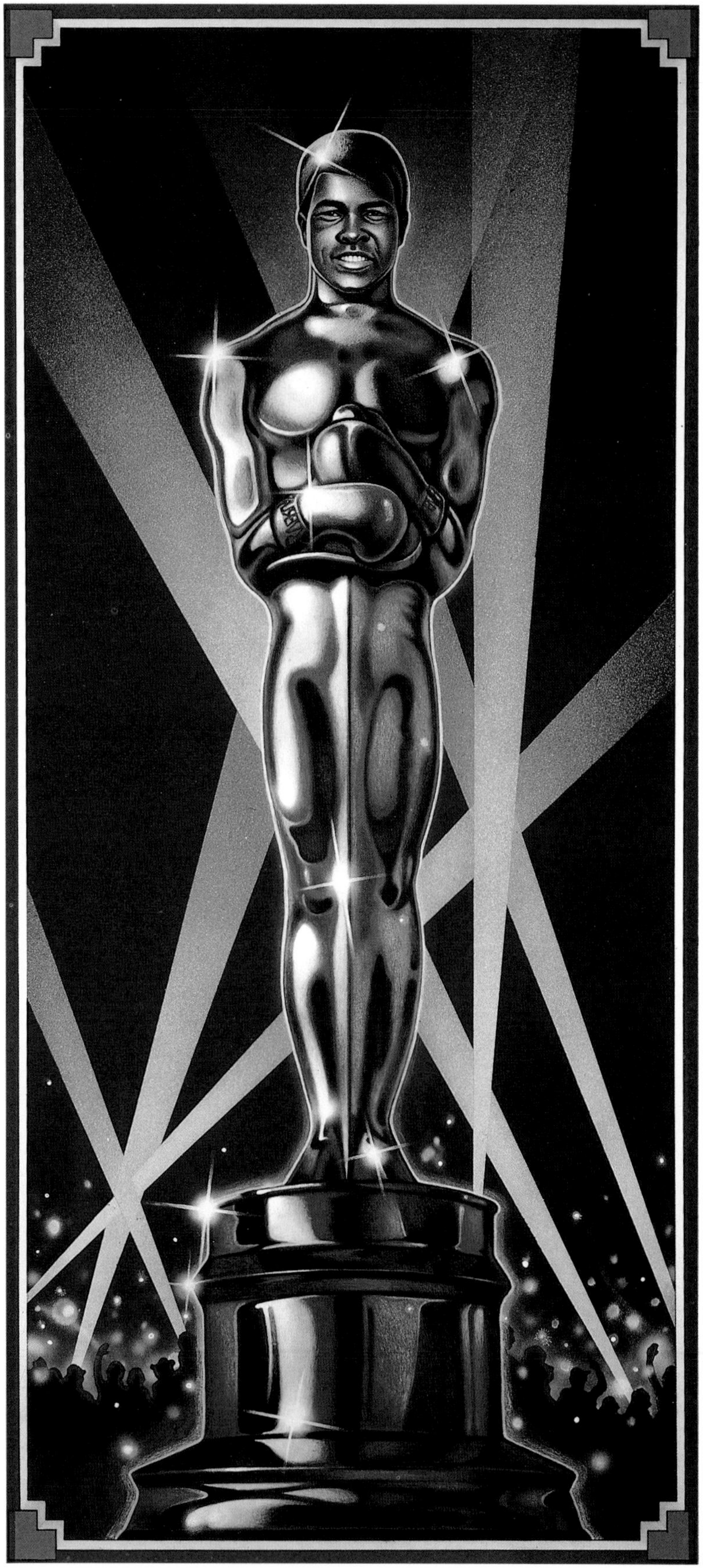

Muhammad Ali *David Edward Byrd 1976*

Elvis *Linda Stokes 1979*

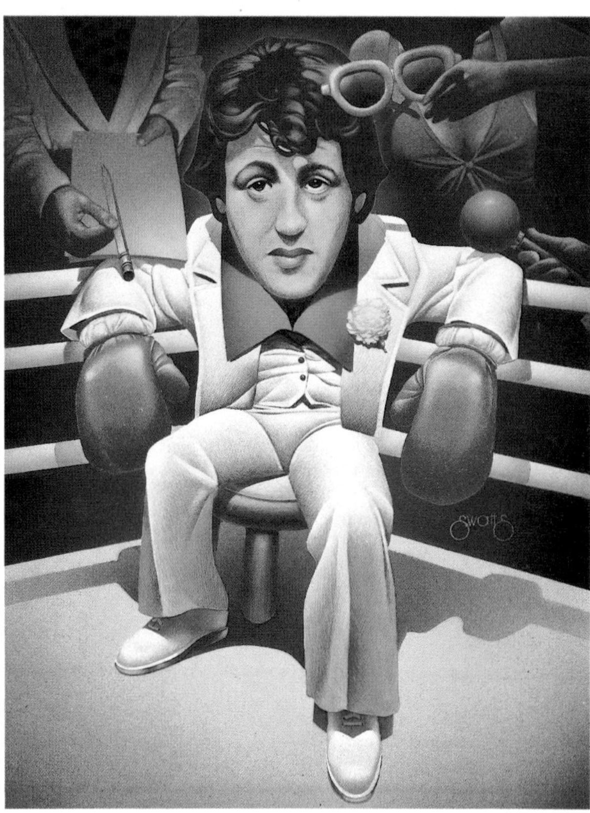

Sylvester Stallone *Stan Watts 1978*

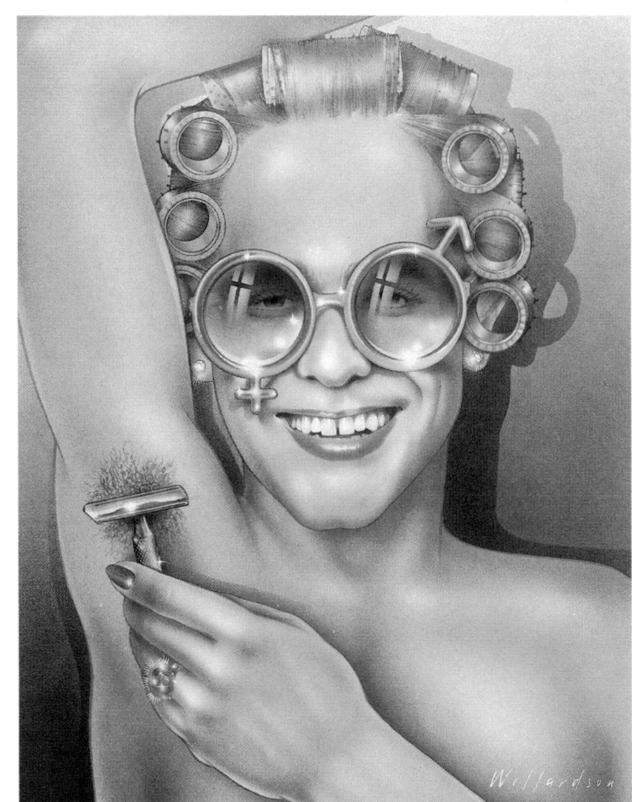

Elton John *David Willardson 1977*

King Tut *Lou Beach 1978*

Meryl Streep *George Stavrinos 1979*

Sissy Spacek *Lisa Powers/Taki Ono 1980*

Sally Field *Richard Amsel 1979*

Diane Keaton *Brian Davis 1977*

Sissy Spacek and Tommy Lee Jones
Richard Amsel 1980

Phil Ochs *John Lykes 1978*

Mozart *Christoph Blumrich 1979*

Tom Waits *Nick Taggart 1976*

Kurt Weill *Christoph Blumrich 1975*

Bruce Springsteen *Kim Whitesides 1975*

George Gershwin *Doug Johnson 1978*

Elvis Costello *Pearl Beach 1979*

Steve Reeves *Joe Morrocco 1979*

Larry Flynt *Joe Heiner 1978*

John Wayne *Christoph Blumrich 1973*

Travolta *Andy Engle 1978*

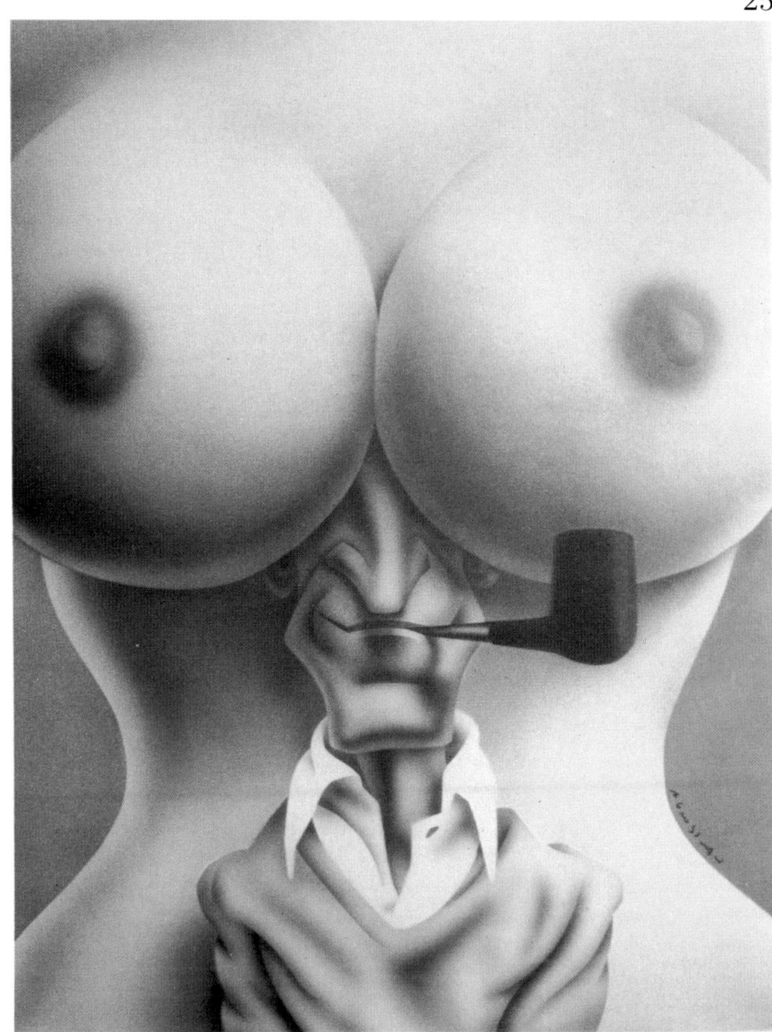

Hugh Hefner *Robert Grossman 1970*

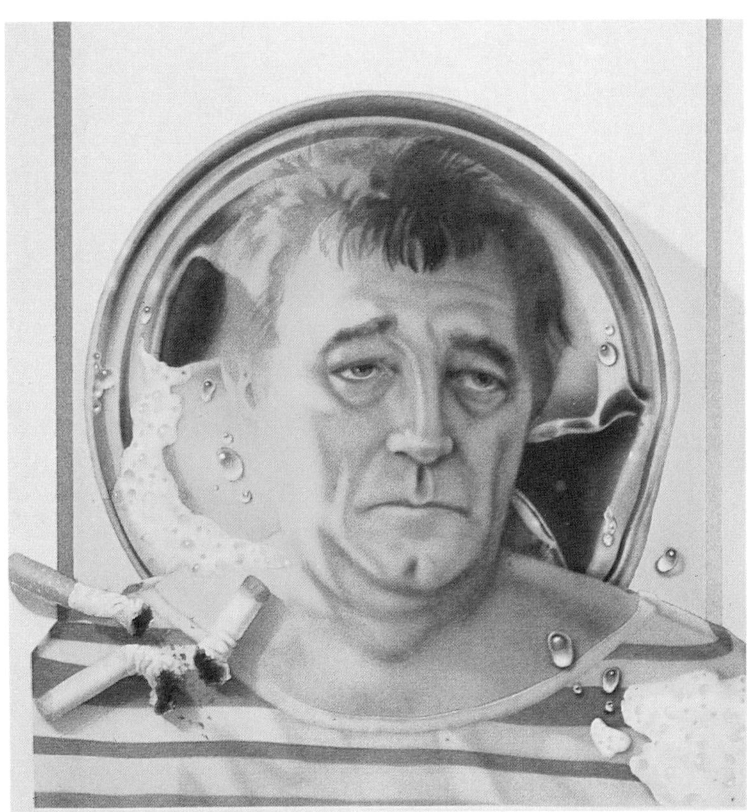

Robert Mitchum *Charles E. White III 1972*

James Dean *Antonio 1976*

Marilyn Monroe *Linda Stokes 1979*

Elvis I *Andy Warhol 1964*

Judy Garland *Lloyd Ziff 1970*

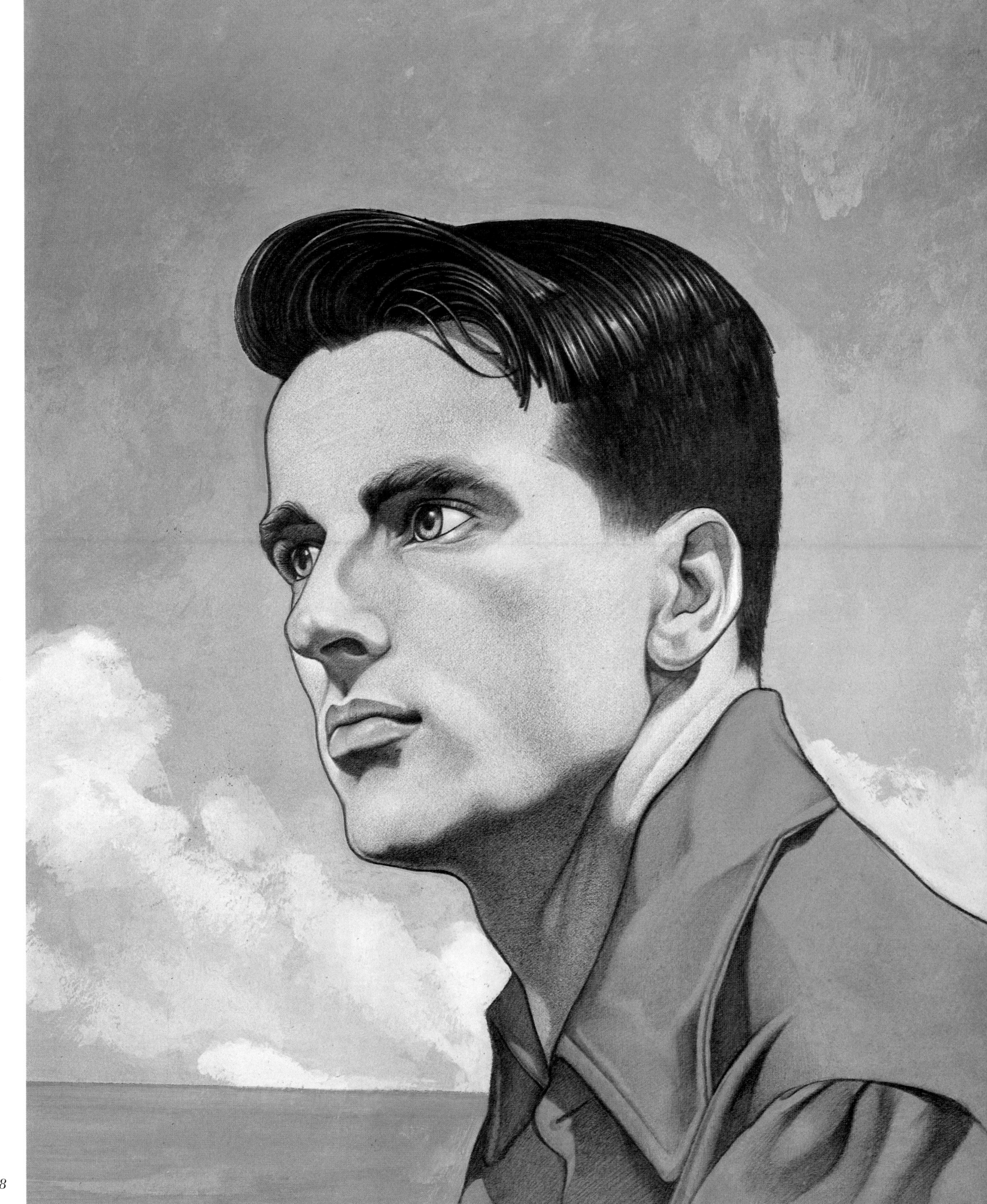

Montgomery Clift
George Stavrinos 1978

Leonard Nimoy *Brian Zick 1979*

Farrah Fawcett *Robert Risko 1978*

Jack Lord *William Rieser 1980*

"Here's Johnny" *Rod Dyer 1980*

Robert Conrad *David Edward Byrd 1978*

Mary Hartman *David Willardson 1976*

Lucy *Richard Amsel 1974*

John Belushi as Liz Taylor *John Andrews 1979*

Gloria Vanderbilt *David Croland 1970*

Pat Ast *Patrick Nagel 1977*

Sayoko *Pater Sato 1974*

Marilyn *Vartan 1980*

Glenn Miller *Bob Zoell 1969*

Louis Armstrong *Pearl Beach 1977*

Ornette Coleman *Steve Miller 1976*

Neil Sedaka
John Van Hamersveld 1976

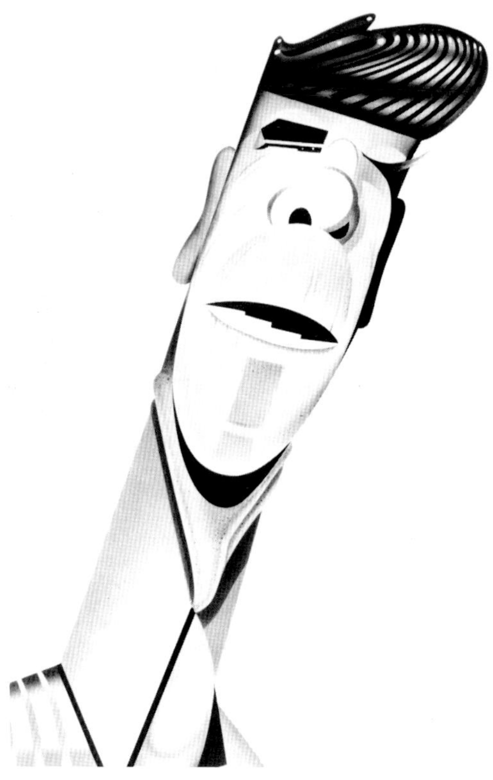

Ronald Reagan *Robert Risko 1980*

George Washington *Wayne McLoughlin 1974*

MacArthur *Philip Slagter 1977*

Jimmy Rotten *Carol Bouman 1978*

Jerry Brown *Linda Stokes 1979*

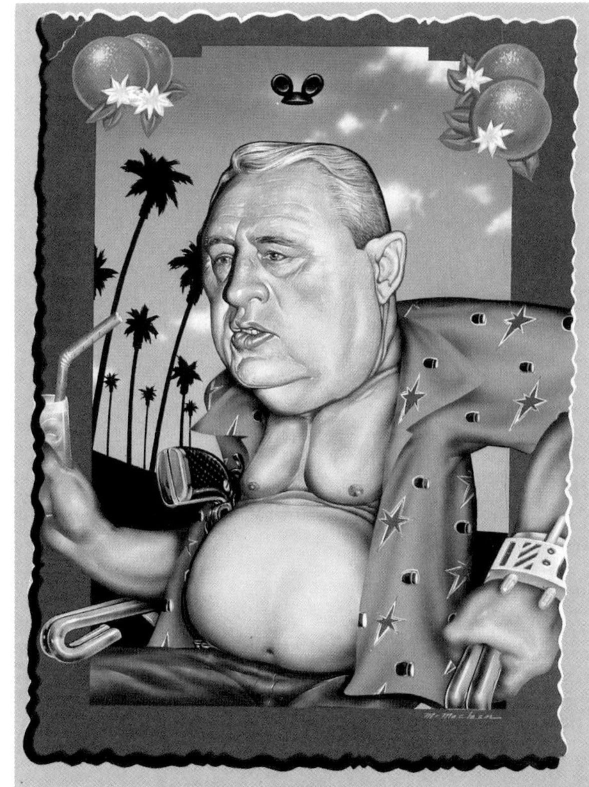

Chief Ed Davis *David McMacken 1978*

Jimmy Carter *Robert Grossman 1977*

Fred Astaire *Kim Whitesides 1972*

Johnny Rotten *James Valentine 1979*

The Simple Supper *John Van Hamersveld 1974*

Larry Flynt *Robert Rodriguez 1977*

Jerry Lewis *Doug Taylor 1978*

Jayne Mansfield *Dale Sizer 1980*

John Wayne *Philip Hays 1972*

Marisa Berenson _Paul Jasmin 1979_

Berry Berenson Perkins _Paul Jasmin 1979_

Liza Minnelli
Richard Bernstein 1979

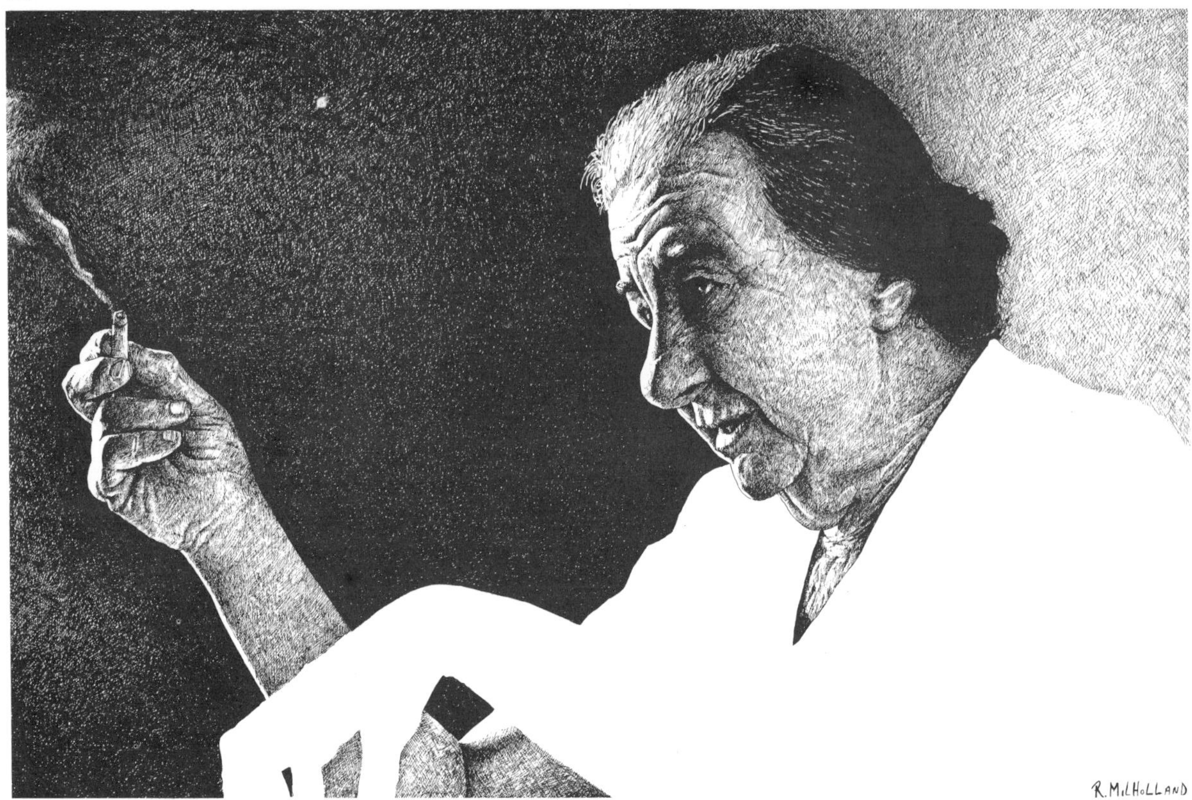

Golda Meir *Richard Milholland 1980*

W.C. Fields *Dennis Mukai 1980*

Mao *Andy Warhol 1972*

Chaplin *Ken Rosenberg 1978*

Castro *Peter Palombi 1975*

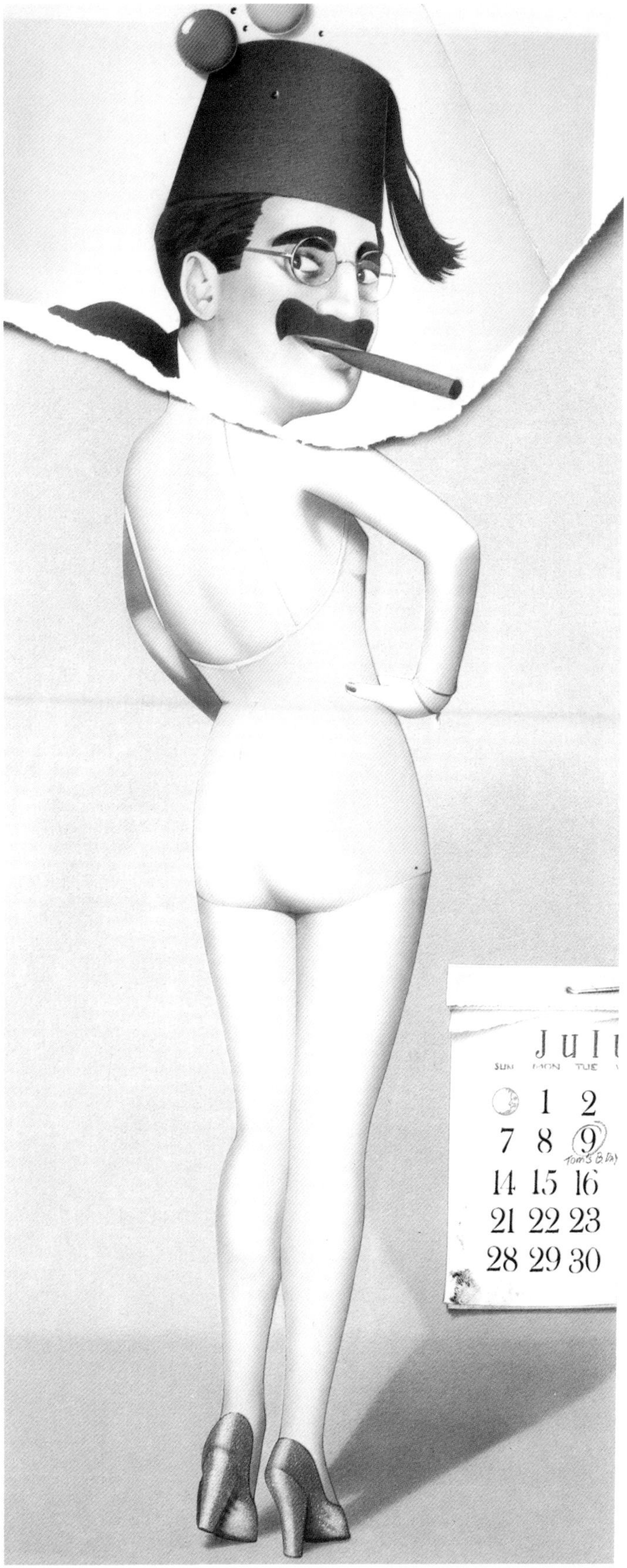

Groucho *Fred Nelson 1980*

Woody Allen *Kathy Staico Schorr 1980*

Mel Brooks *Don Weller 1976*

Martin Mull *Brian Zick 1979*

Steve Martin *William Rieser 1978*

Lorne Michaels *David McMacken 1978*

Gilda Radner *William Rieser 1978*

Chevy Chase *Stan Watts 1979*

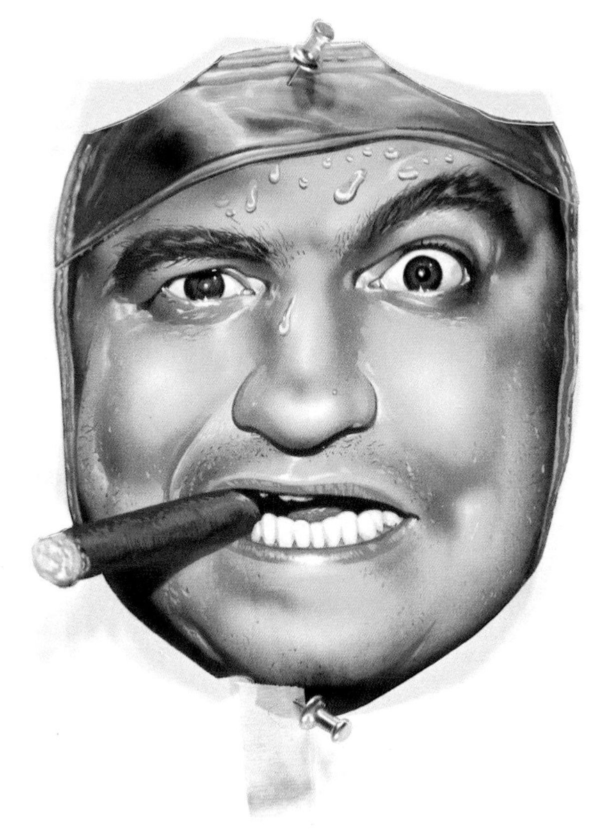

John Belushi *David McMacken 1979*

Buddy Holly *David Willardson 1979*

Elvis *Joe Stewart 1980*

Jerry Lee Lewis
Mick Haggerty 1978 ➤

Gene Vincent *Mick Haggerty 1976*

Fabian *David McMacken 1970*

Arnold Schwarzenegger *David Willardson 1973*

Joe Namath *Robert Grossman 1972*

Jimmy Connors *David Willardson 1974*

"Mean" Joe Greene *Dickran Palulian 1976*

Max Baer *Dickran Palulian 1978*

O.J. Simpson *John Hamagami 1979*

Mark Spitz *David Willardson 1973*

James Dean *John Van Hamersveld 1974*

The Misfits *Tim Clark 1975*

Dolly and Marlon *Randy South 1979*

Fred and Rita *Richard Bernstein 1976*

Woody Allen *Ron Lieberman 1978*

Mel Brooks *Barry Phillips 1978*

Young John Wayne *Victor Stabin 1978*

Salvador Dali *Stephen Durke 1976*

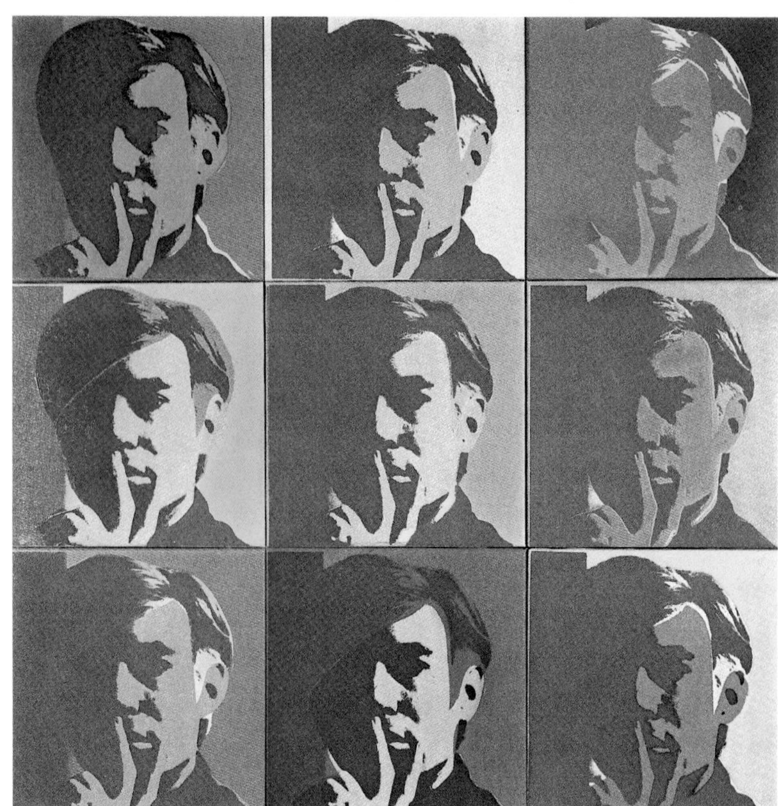

Self-Portrait *Andy Warhol 1966*

Disney, Picasso, and Warhol *Richard Bernstein 1978*

David Hockney *Joe Morrocco 1979*

Van Gogh
Bob Zoell 1979

Elvis Costello *Lou Brooks 1979*

Bob Marley *Mick Haggerty 1976*

The Who *Gary Panter 1979*

DEVO *Bob Zoell 1980*

Rod Stewart *Charles E. White III 1973*

Santa Claus *Doug Johnson 1974*

Gore Vidal *Barry Phillips 1978*

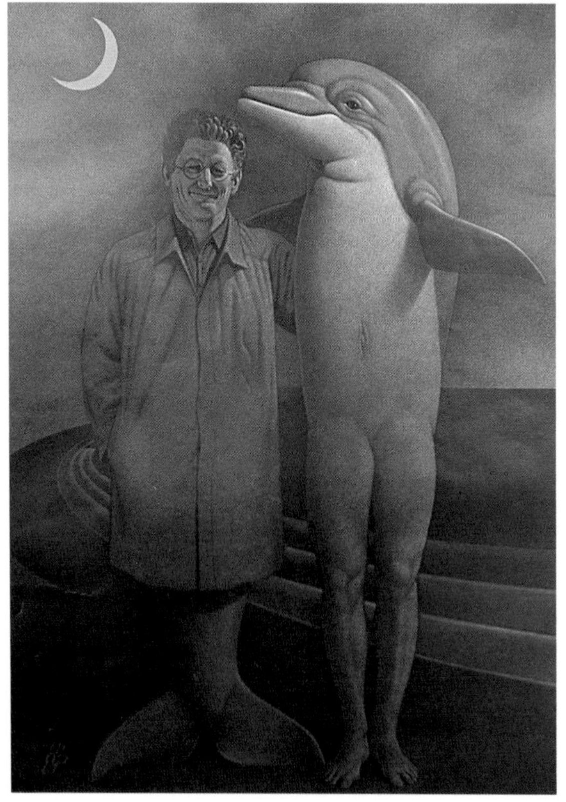

Dr. John Lilly *Don Ivan Punchatz 1973*

Dr. Joyce Brothers *Cathy Barancik 1980*

François Truffaut *Debbie Kuhn 1979*

Buckminster Fuller *Jim Heimann 1977*

Timothy Leary *Cynthia Marsh 1977*

Donna Summer *Robert Risko 1978*

The Village People *Lou Brooks 1979*

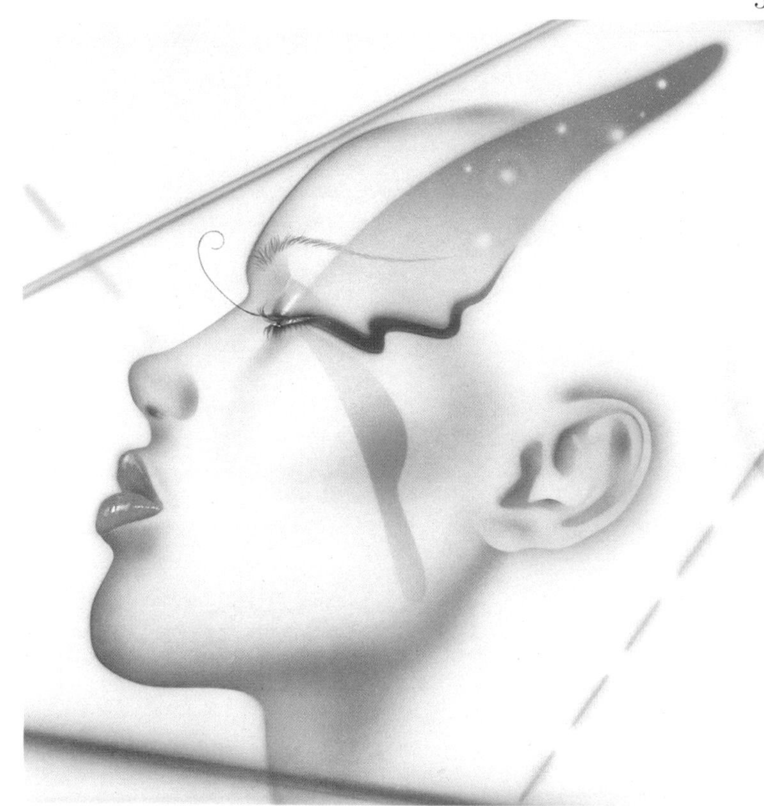

Grace Jones *Pater Sato 1977*

Marilyn *Antonio 1977*

Liza Minnelli and Robert De Niro *Richard Amsel 1977*

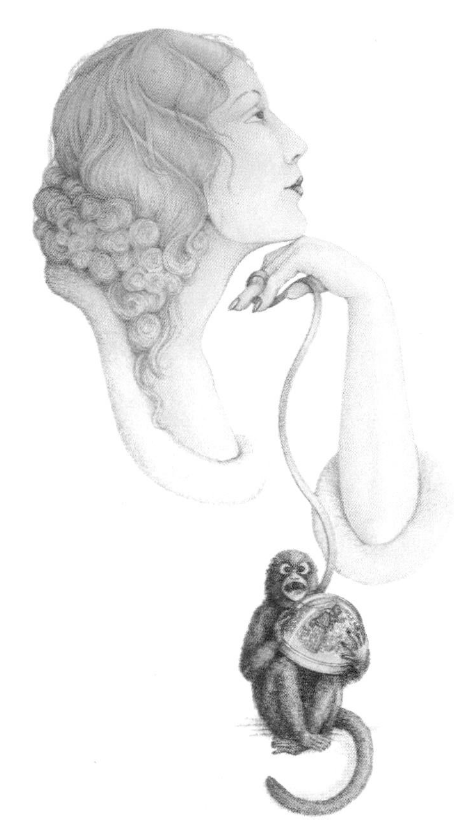

Fay Wray *Heather Taylor 1980*

Charlie and Herb *Tim Clark 1975*

Barbara Stanwyck and Fred MacMurray *Steve Carver 1979*

Clark Gable and Vivien Leigh *Richard Amsel 1976*

Burt Duck and Deborah Duck *Neon Park 1977*

Bogart *Nick Taggart 1976*

Henry Fonda *Lisa Powers/Taki Ono 1980*

Elvis at 50 *Philip Hays 1977*

Marilyn at 50 *Philip Hays 1977*

Katharine Hepburn *Richard Amsel 1979*

John Wayne *Stan Watts 1979*

Peter Allen *John Van Hamersveld 1976*

Pearl Bailey *Nicholas Gaetano 1974*

The Village People *Robert Risko 1979*

Pavarotti *Tim Lewis 1980*

Diana Ross and Berry Gordy *Mick Haggerty 1977*

Impersonating Elvis *Todd Schorr 1978*

Zorro *Brian Zick 1979*

The Lone Ranger *John Hamagami 1980*

Roy, Dale, and Trigger *David Willardson 1970*

Hopalong Cassidy *Tommy Steele 1973*

Flash Gordon *Todd Schorr 1980*

Donald Byrd *Steve Miller 1976*

Dizzy Gillespie *Les Katz 1978*

Stanley Clarke *Robert Giusti 1976*

John Klemmer *Joe Garnett 1978*

Anita O'Day *Patricia Dryden 1978*

Billie Holiday *Pearl Beach 1977*

Billie Holiday *Doug Johnson 1973*

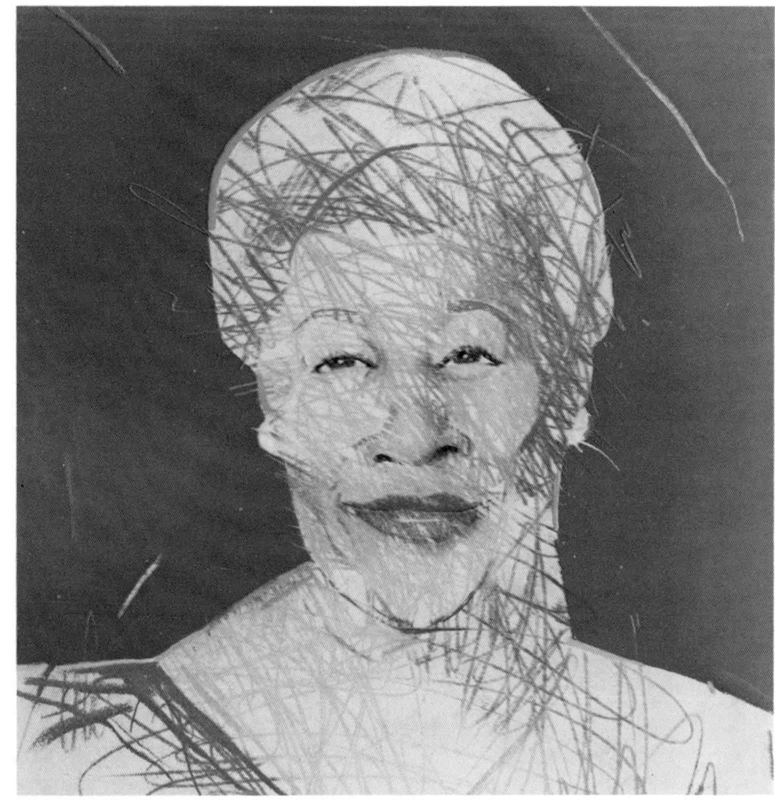

Ella Fitzgerald *Patricia Dryden 1978*

Jimmy Carter *Dickran Palulian 1979*

John F. Kennedy *Stephen Durke 1978*

Gerald Ford *Don Ivan Punchatz 1974*

Ted Kennedy *Robert Risko 1980*

John Connally *Stephen Durke 1979*

Uncle Sam *Tim Lewis 1979*

Ronald Reagan *Robert Grossman 1967*

Liza Minnelli *Antonio 1972*

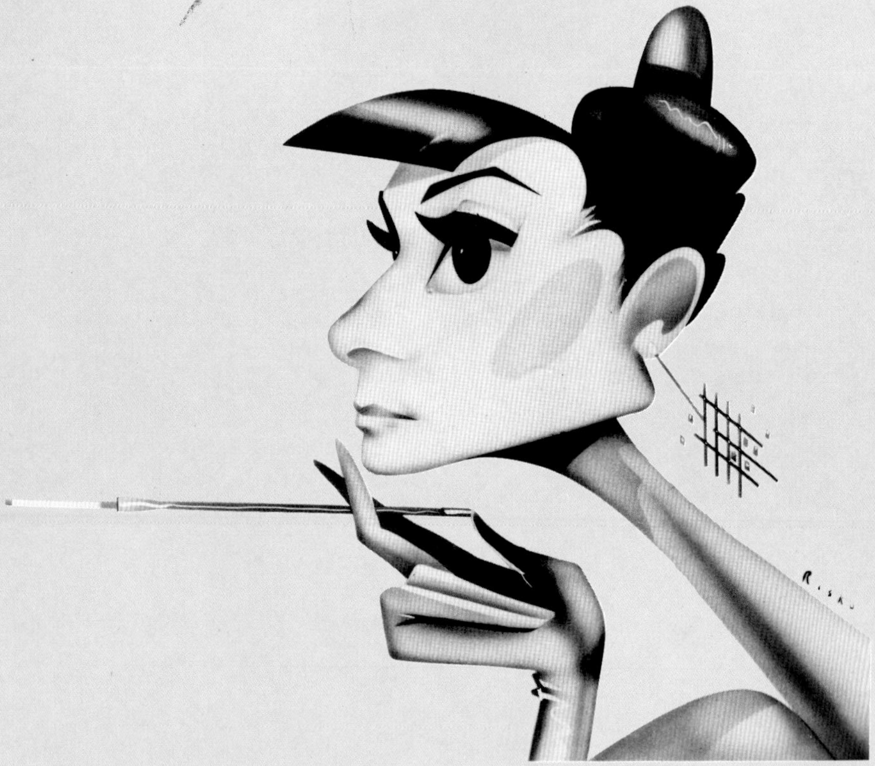

Audrey Hepburn *Robert Risko 1979*

Katharine Hepburn *David Juniper 1979*

Catherine Deneuve *David Croland 1979*

Jack Nicholson *Kim Whitesides 1975*

Stallone *Andy Engle 1978*

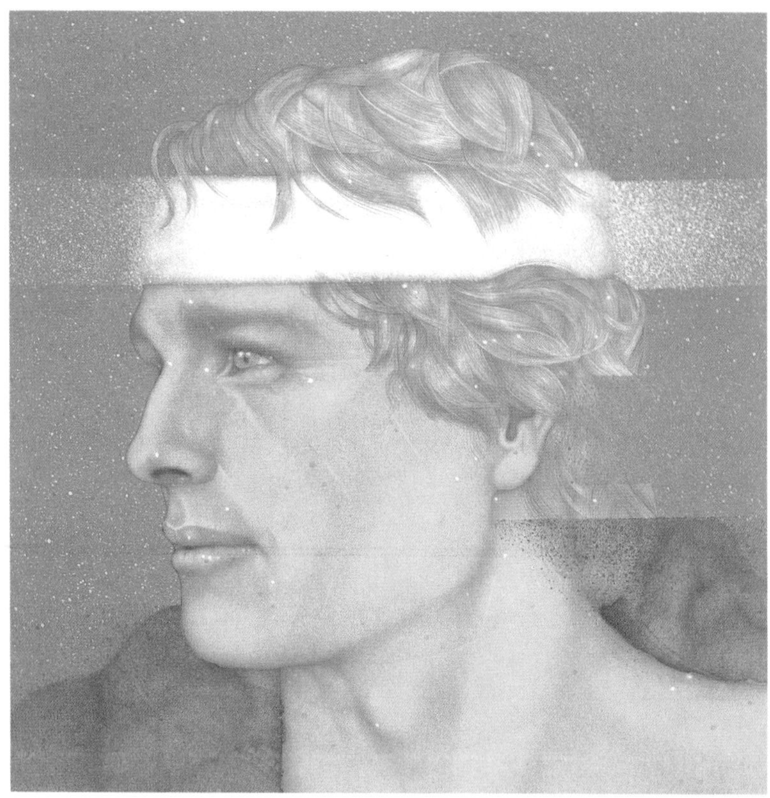

Ryan O'Neal *Mel Odom 1980*

Richard Gere *Rich Mahon 1980*

James Caan *Cynthia Marsh 1978*

John Travolta *Linda Stokes 1979*

Robert De Niro *Richard Amsel 1976*

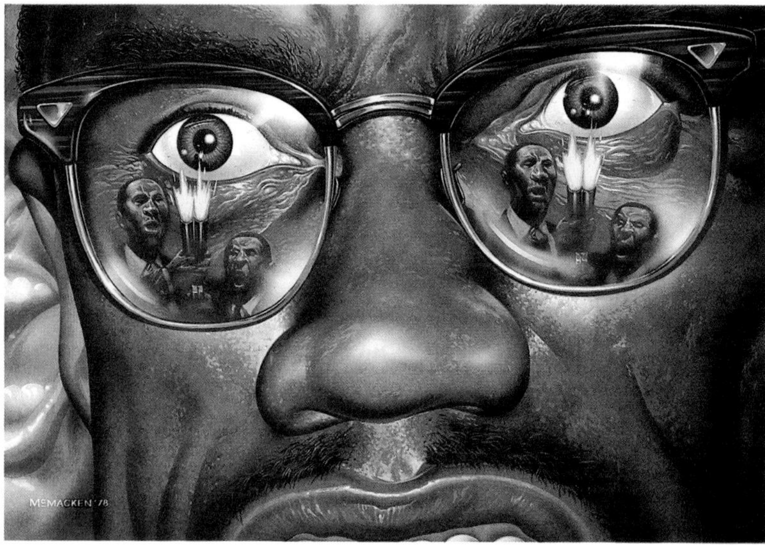

Malcolm X *David McMacken 1979*

Gregg Allman *Stan Watts 1979*

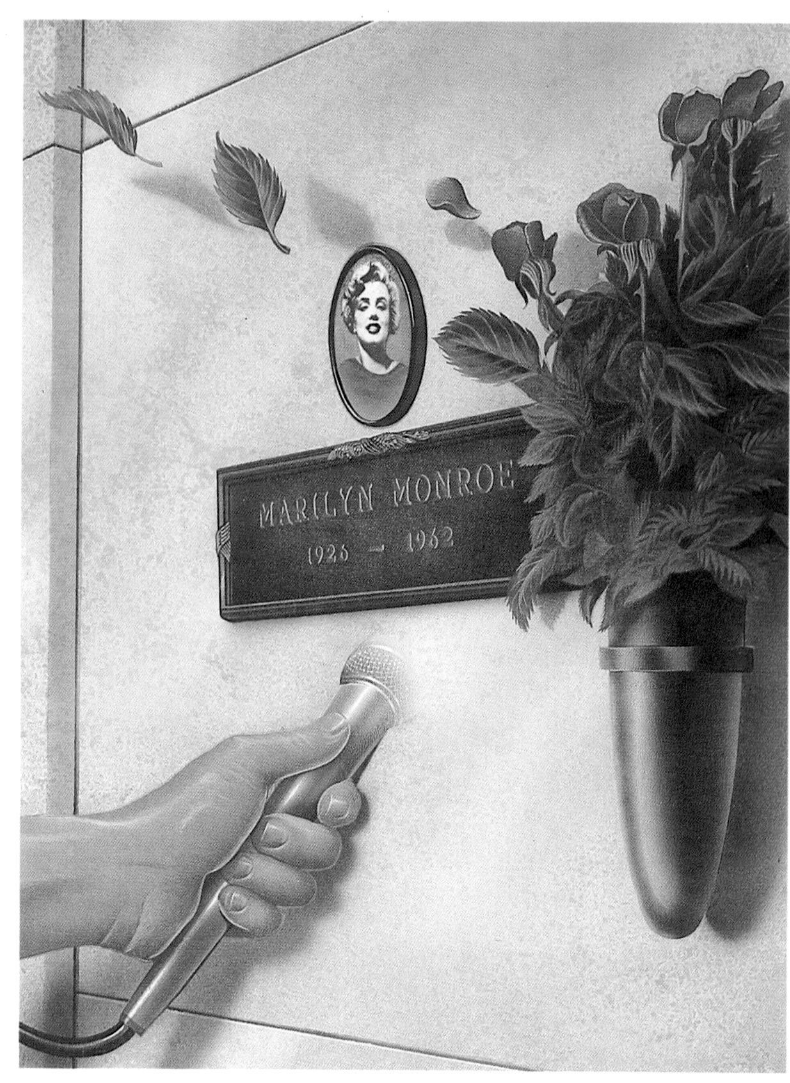

Marilyn *Barry Phillips 1980*

John Wayne *Todd Schorr 1978*

At Home with J.F.K. *Ron Lieberman 1973*

Johnny Winter *Richard Shaefer, William King, and Basil Pao 1975*

Diana Ross *Dennis Mukai 1978*

Janis Joplin *Steve Miller 1975*

Brian Wilson *Kim Whitesides 1976*

Elton John *Don Weller 1974*

Blondie *Kim Whitesides 1979*

The Ramones *Mick Haggerty 1977*

Billy Joel *Robert Giusti 1979*

Burt Reynolds *Joe Garnett 1978*

Peter Sellers *Richard Bernstein 1980*

Marlon Brando
William Shirley 1974 ➤

Jon Voight *Kim Whitesides 1978*

John Travolta *Paul Jasmin 1980*

Richard Pryor *Stephen Durke 1980*

Lily Tomlin and Art Carney *Richard Amsel 1977*

Lily Tomlin *Cynthia Marsh 1976*

Chevy Chase *Andy Engle 1978*

Lily Tomlin *Ron Lieberman 1977*

Phyllis Diller *Doug Taylor 1978*

Mary Hartman *David Edward Byrd 1974*

Laverne, Shirley, and producer Garry Marshall *David McMacken 1979*

Lucy and Desi *William Grant 1980*

Farrah Fawcett *Brian Zick 1978*

Mary Duck *Neon Park 1977*

Norman Lear *John Lykes 1978*

Dinah! *Cathy Barancik 1980*

John Travolta *Richard Amsel 1978*

Esther Williams *Lisa Powers/Taki Ono 1979*

Lolita *Bill Murphy 1974*

Franco Columbu *Richard Milholland 1978*

Raquel Welch *Richard Bernstein 1975*

Jim Morrison *Cynthia Marsh 1978*

Fats Domino *Tim Clark 1971*

Deborah Harry *Todd Curtis 1980*

Bob Dylan *John Van Hamersveld 1978*

Peter Tosh *Doug Johnson 1979*

Ricky Nelson *Bob Zoell 1971*

Talking Heads *Mick Haggerty 1980*

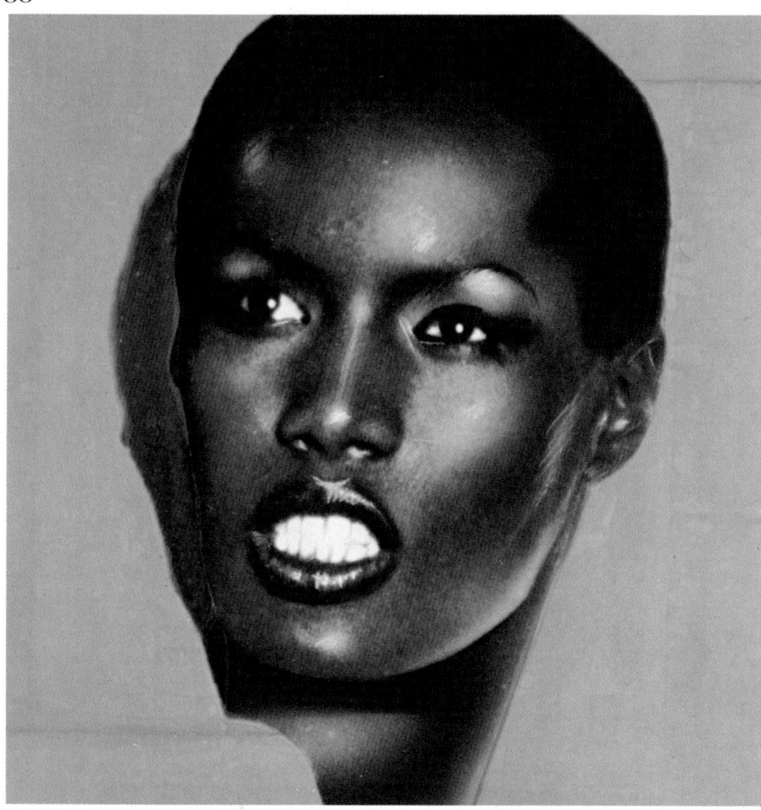

Grace Jones *Richard Bernstein 1977*

Grace Jones *Richard Bernstein 1978*

Grace Jones *Richard Bernstein 1978*

Grace Jones *Richard Bernstein 1979*

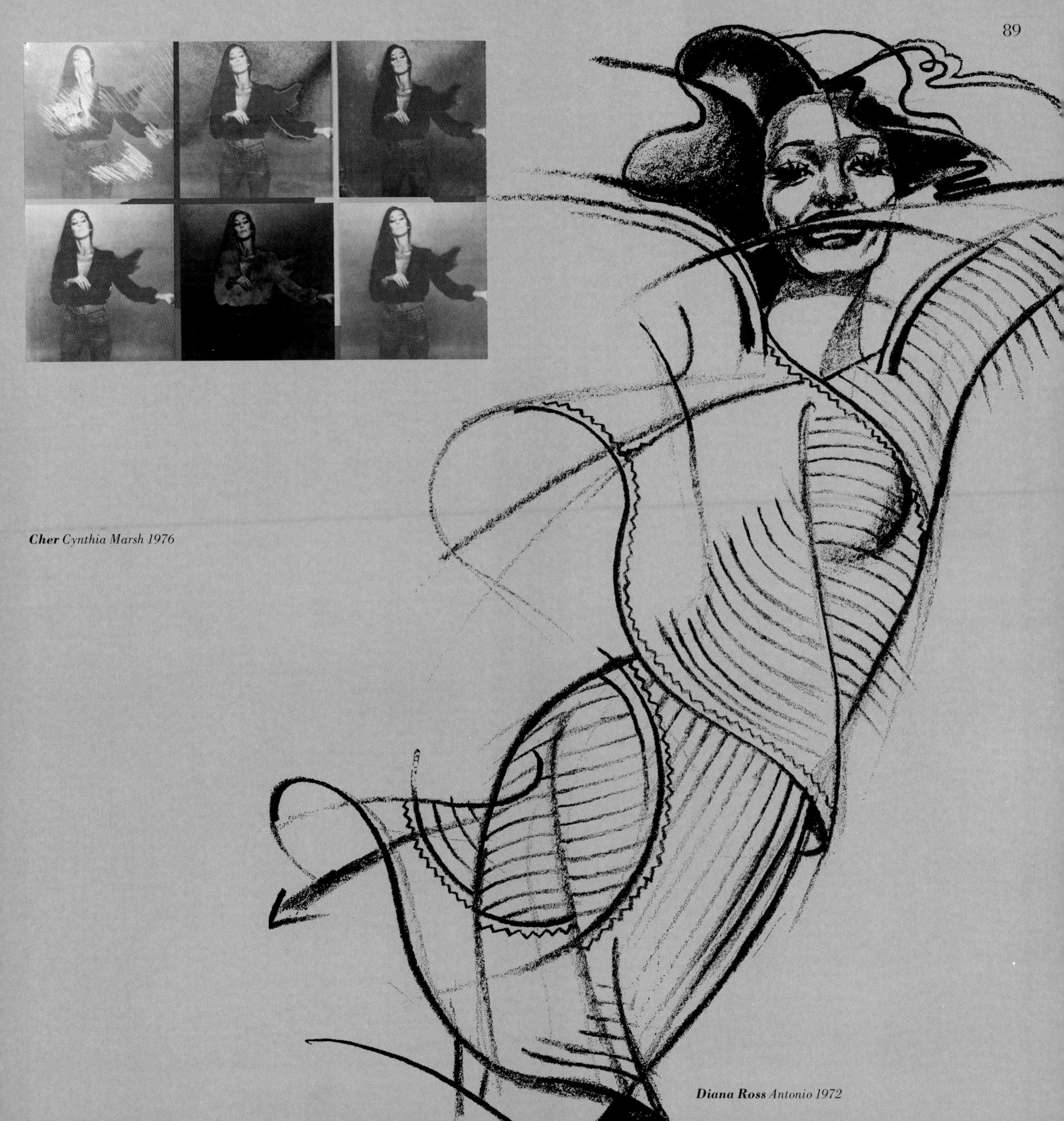

Cher *Cynthia Marsh 1976*

Diana Ross *Antonio 1972*

Aunt J *Tommy Steele 1980*

Barry Manilow and Bagel *David Willardson 1976*

"Wild Bill" Hickok *Jean Paul Goude 1975*

Elizabeth II Anticipating Bloomingdale's *Philip Slagter 1977*

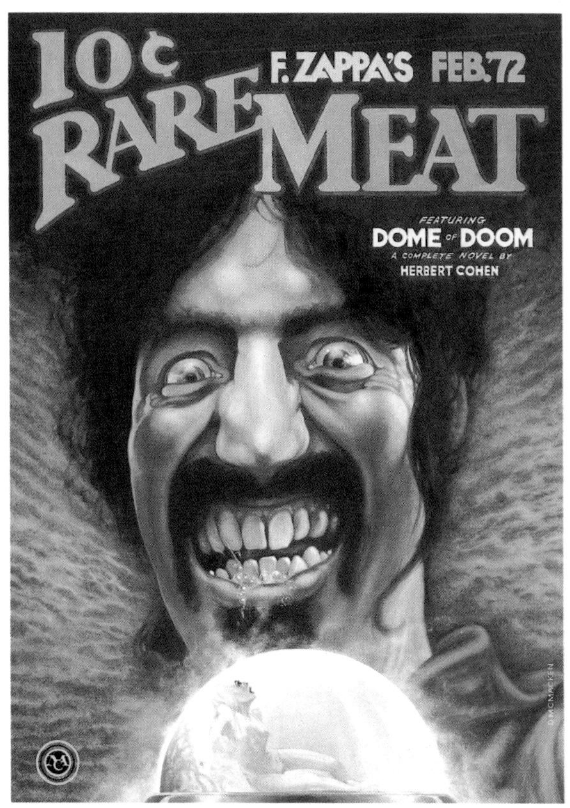

Frank Zappa *David McMacken 1972*

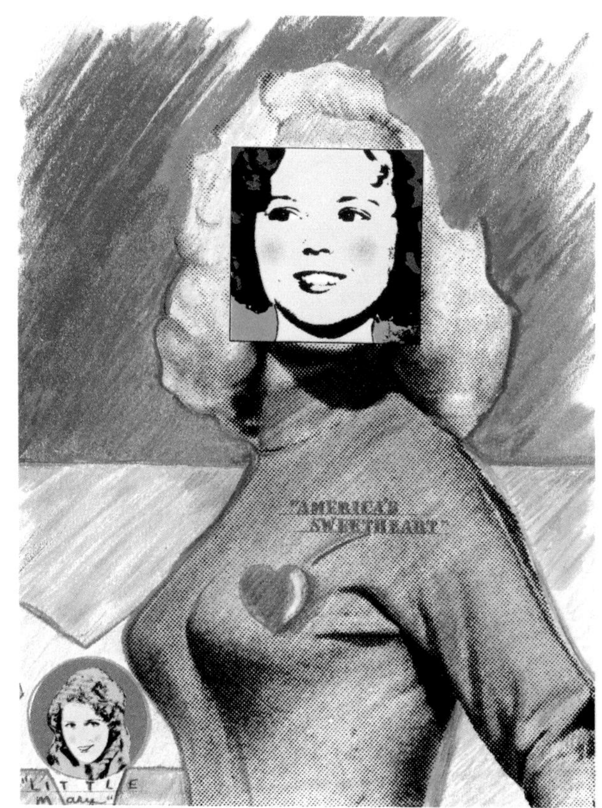

"Little Shirley" *Jim Heimann 1977*

Sherlock Holmes *Nicholas Gaetano 1977*

Billy Carter *John Lykes 1979*

Jean Harlow *William Shirley 1973*

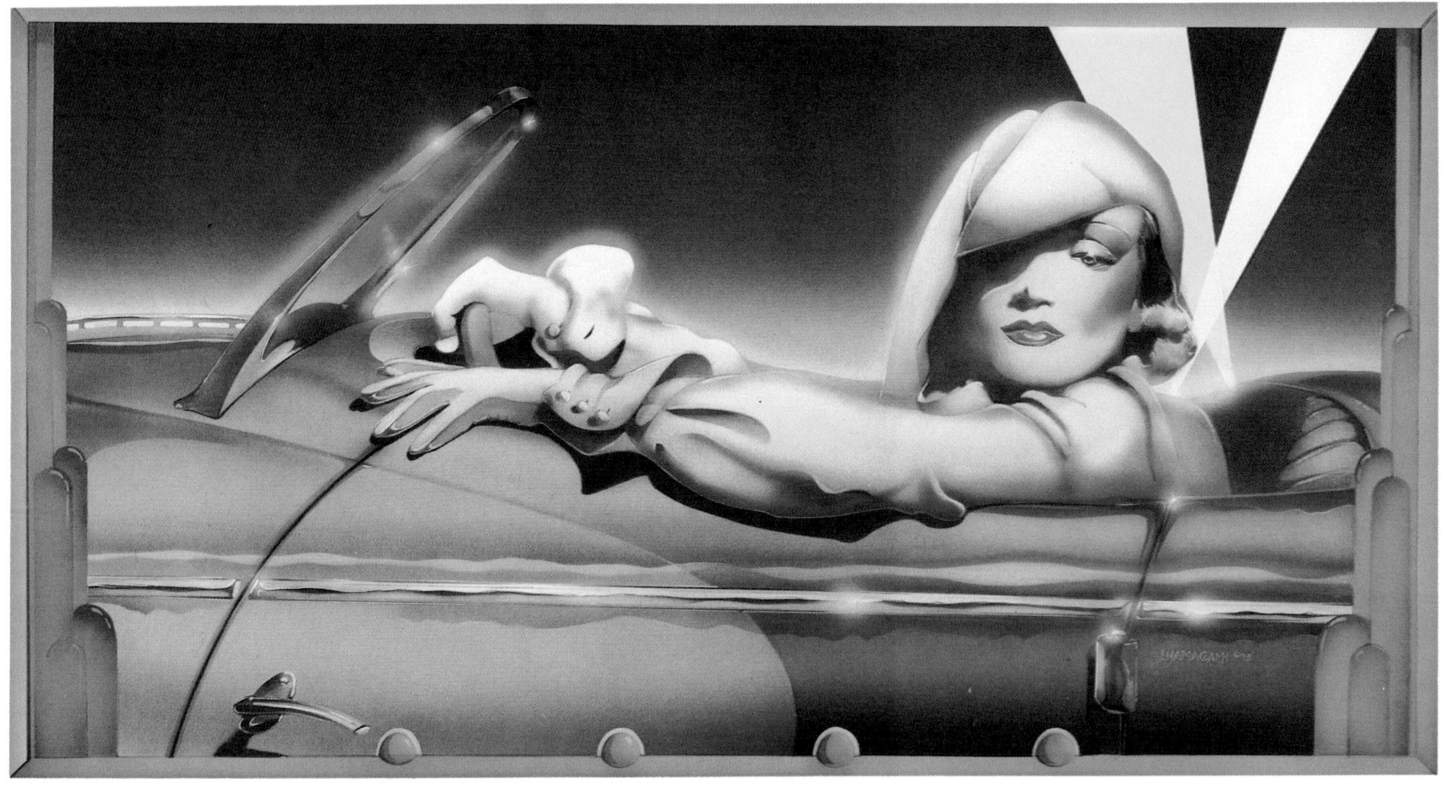

Marlene Dietrich *John Hamagami 1978*

Clark Gable *Nancy Stahl 1978*

Joan Crawford *David Croland 1979*

Dietrich *James Valentine 1975*

Idi Amin *Debbie Kuhn 1978*

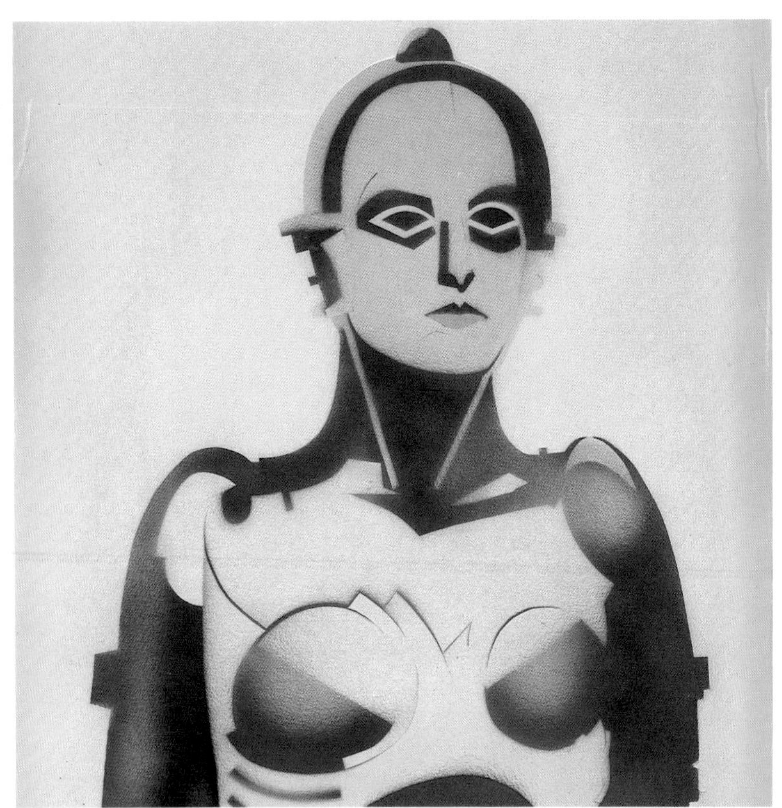

Ultima Efficiency *Gary Panter 1980*

J. Paul Getty III *Justin Carroll 1977*

Jim Jones *Philip Hays 1979* ➤

PHILIP HAYS

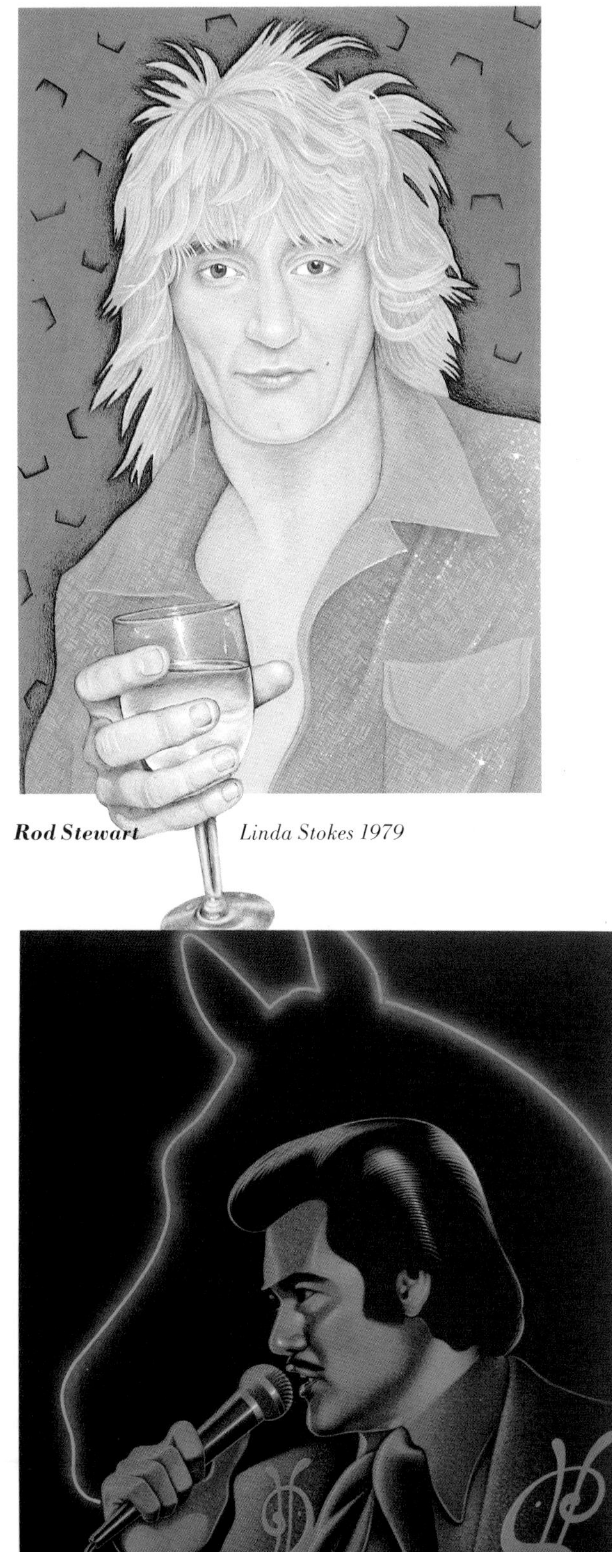

Rod Stewart *Linda Stokes 1979*

Billy Joel *Dickran Palulian 1979*

Wayne Newton *Robert Giusti 1980*

Bing Crosby *John Hamagami 1978*

Ray Charles *Ron Kriss 1976*

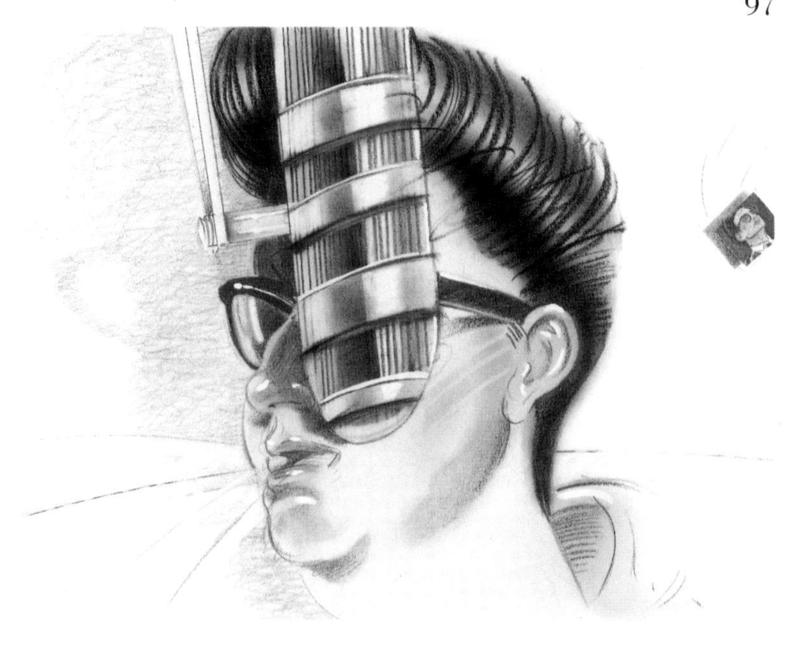

Roy Orbison *William Rieser 1980*

David Bowie *Robert Risko 1976*

Muddy Waters *Dickran Palulian 1975*

Betty Page *Bette Levine 1979*

Linda Ronstadt *Kim Whitesides 1978*

Ann Miller *Jeff Wack 1980*

Cathy Chamberlain *Ron Lieberman 1976*

Betty Page (Nutrix #2) *Robert Blue 1977*

Bette Midler *Richard Amsel 1975*

Neil Young *Kim Whitesides 1972*

Stevie Wonder *Doug Johnson 1979*

Bob Dylan
Kim Whitesides 1974 ➤

Peter Frampton *Steve Miller 1976*

Billy Joel *Charles E. White III 1979*

WHITESIDES

Jackie Kennedy Onassis *Antonio 1973*

Rona Barrett *David Croland 1979*

Barbra Streisand *Robert Grossman 1975*

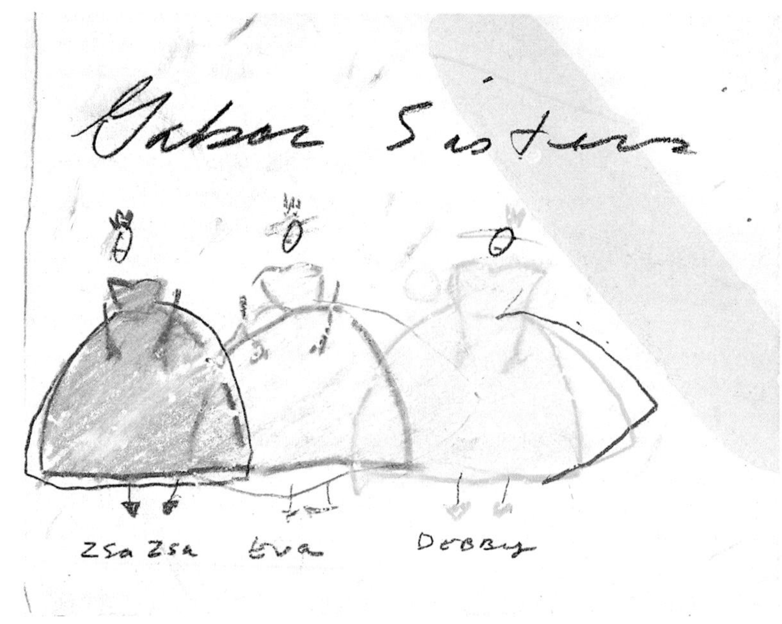

The Gabor Sisters *Cathy Barancik 1980*

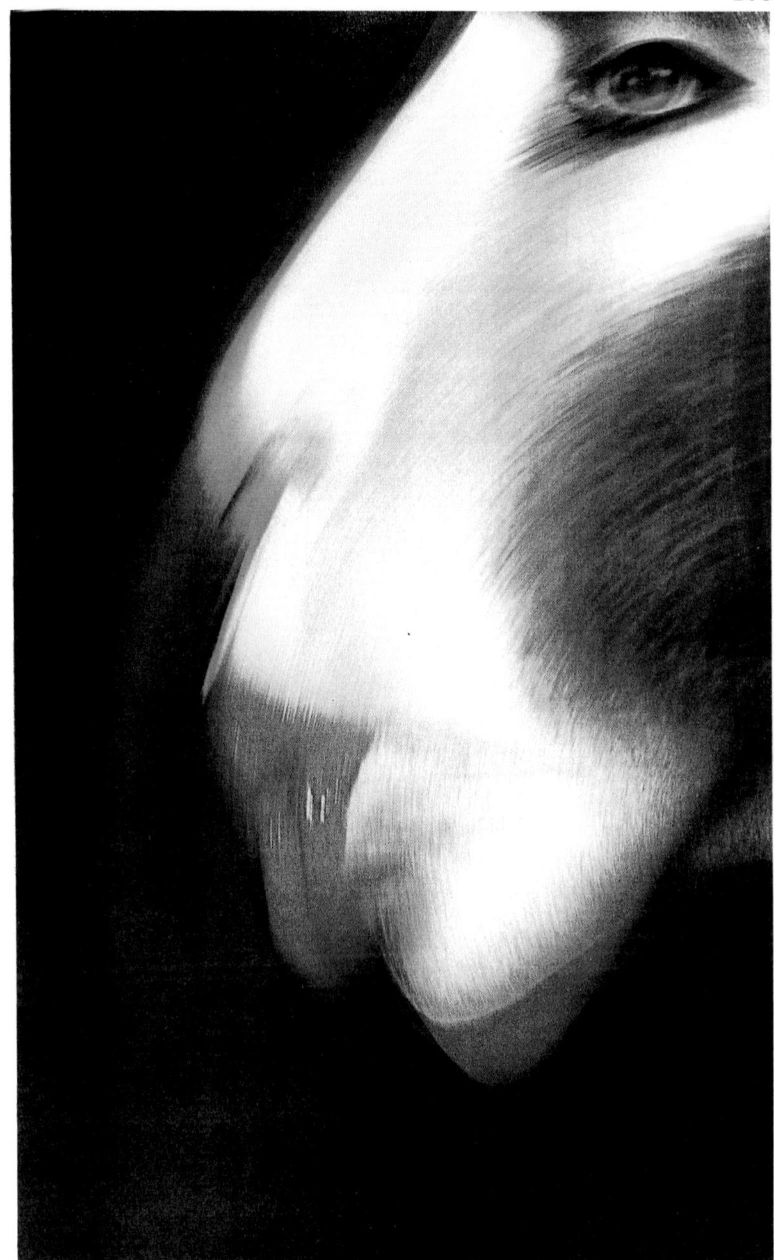

Deborah Harry *Richard Bernstein 1979*

Streisand *Lou Beach 1979*

Bonnie Pointer *Brian Davis 1979*

Bob Dylan *William Shirley 1980*

Jerry Lee Lewis *Philip Hays 1980*

Elvis *Dan Quarnstrom 1978*

Rod Stewart *Cynthia Marsh 1978*

Zappa *Nick Taggart 1975*

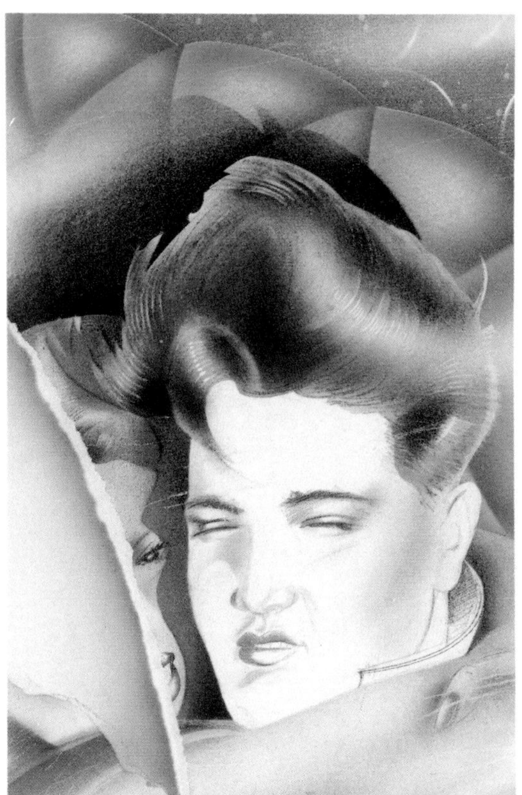

Elvis *William Rieser 1980*

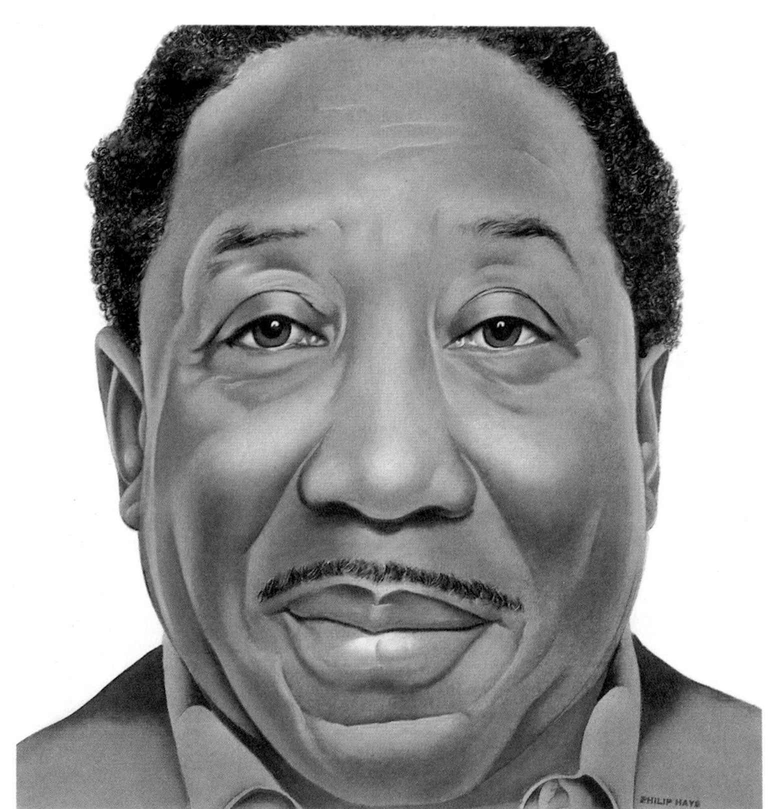

Muddy Waters *Philip Hays 1978*

Humphrey Bogart *Vincent Topazio 1977*

Humphrey Duck *Neon Park 1977*

Charlie Chan *David McMacken 1980*

Telly Savalas *Dennis Mukai 1978*

James Garner *Cynthia Marsh*

Einstein *Gary Cooley 1977*

Divine *Patrick Nagel 1977*

Divine *William Rieser 1978*

Divine *Richard Bernstein 1980*

Einstein *Doug Johnson 1979*

Einstein *Dennis Mukai 1979*

Gay Talese *Doug Johnson 1973*

The Creature *Neon Park 1976*

King Kong *Steve Miller 1976*

Elvis Zombie *Gary Panter 1980*

Castro *Tim Lewis 1979*

Howard Hughes *Fred Nelson 1979*

Barbra Streisand *William Shirley 1974*

Einstein *Charles E. White III 1973*

Diana Ross *David Croland 1978*

Judy Collins *Richard Milholland 1979*

Bette Midler *Richard Amsel 1972*

Linda Ronstadt *David Willardson 1977* ➤

Nixon *David McMacken 1972*

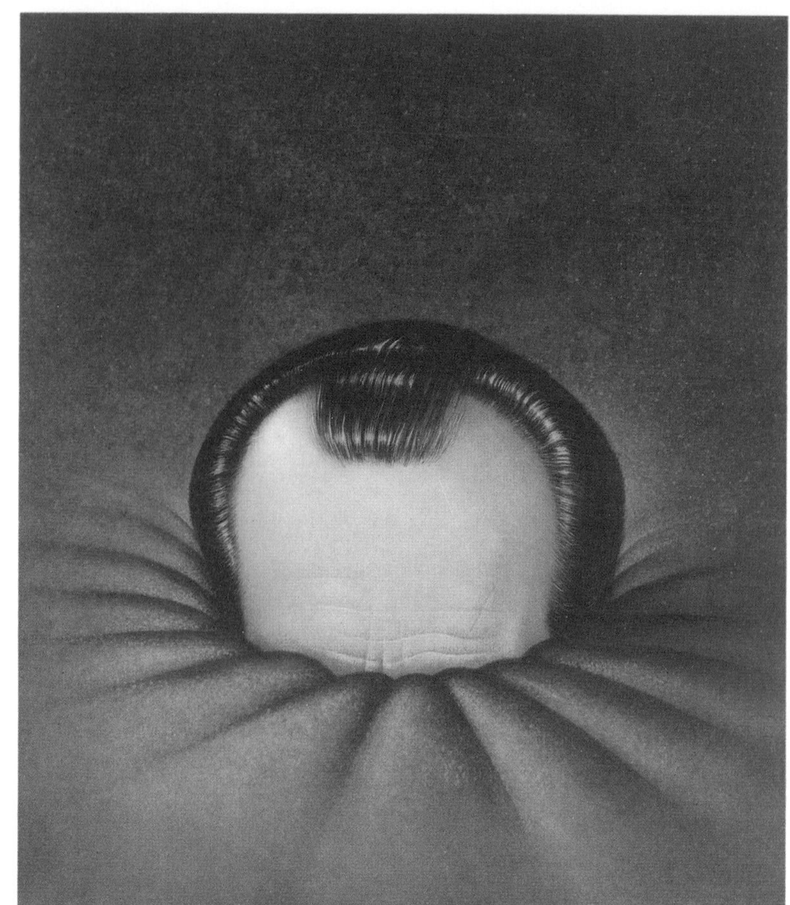

Henry Kissinger *Lou Beach 1977*

Nixon *David Wilcox 1974*

Nixon and Kissinger *George Stavrinos 1976*

G. Gordon Liddy *Steve Miller 1977*

Lou Reed *David Edward Byrd 1975*

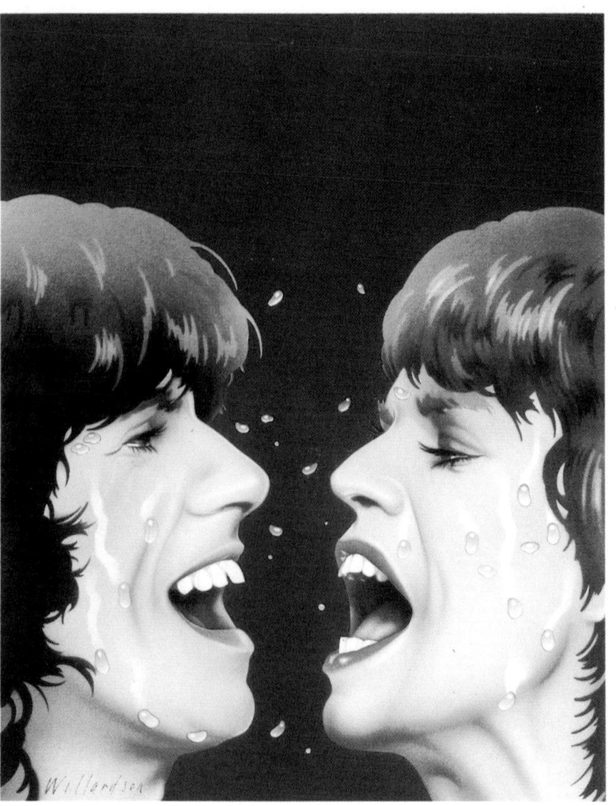

Richard and Jagger *David Willardson 1975*

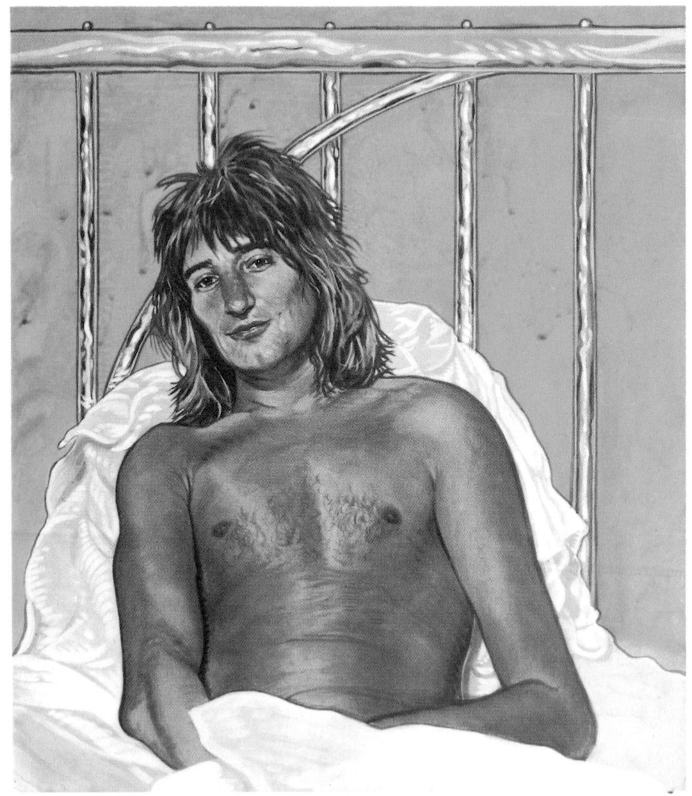

Rod Stewart *Les Katz 1979*

Bruce Springsteen *Dickran Palulian 1979*

David Bowie *Patricia Dryden 1980*

Elton John *Lou Brooks 1978*

Lou Reed *Robert Risko 1976*

Smokey Robinson *Brian Zick 1978*

Jayne Duck *Neon Park 1977*

Betty Duck *Neon Park 1977*

Jane Duck *Neon Park 1977*

Marilyn Duck
Neon Park 1978

Acknowledgments

Andresen Typographics
Young H. Lim and Irene Kairez, G.P. Color
Stat House
Wilcopy
Newell Color Lab
Charlie Wild
Karl Bornstein, Mirage Gallery
Acard Co.
A.G.I.
Don and Linda Berman
Phil Morrison, C.S.U.N.
Johnny Lee
Ken Mowry and Teri Cerino, S.P.N.B.
Ron Allcott, Sound Center
Steve Samiof, STUFF
Ed Taylor
Richard Amsel
Paul Jasmin
Ron Lieberman
Grace Jones
Divine
Richard Bernstein
Michael Fink
Jennifer Shaefer
Vicki Morgan
Pat Yamashiro
Miya Vandover
Chantal Cloutier
Katie Miller
Laird Tyler Fleming
Karin Burkhard
Rick Chalek
Dana Eakin
Jack and Joan
Sparkie

Harmony Books:
Bruce Harris
Peter Shriver
Ken Sansone
Manuela Soares
Murray Schwartz
Esther Mitgang
Kerry Doyle

Paul and Elaine
Ron
Steffy
Stan and Mitzi
Bill and Estelle
Russ and Hillary
Martin and Edith
Woody
Maurice
Barry
Chris
Debbie
Linda
Fred and Sandy
Terry and Lucy
Karen
Robert
Xtian
Kristina
Bill and Jean
Todd and Kathy
Mike and Cindy
Lou and Clare
Tommy
Jim and Roleen
Vartan and Natasha
Rod and Jackie
Dave and Judy
Dave and Sandy
Charlie and Linda
Rick and Jennifer
Eric and Michelle
Frank and Beth
Bob
Lou and Pearl
Neon
Richard
Bobby
Valentina
Jon, Ada, Matt, and Evie
Joan Love Allemand

Thank You

Special Thanks

I would like to thank the following for their cooperation and assistance:

Interview Magazine
Playboy Magazine
Oui Magazine
A&M Records
CBS Records
Paramount Pictures
Warner Bros. Pictures
MCA/Universal
Hustler Magazine
Chic Magazine
Time Magazine
Sports Illustrated Magazine
T V Guide
New York Magazine
New West Magazine
Esquire Magazine
GQ Magazine
Los Angeles Magazine
Casablanca Records
Island Records
Verve Records
United Artists Records
RCA Records
London Records
Motown Records
WEA Records
Playgirl Magazine
Rolling Stone Magazine
National Lampoon Magazine
Art Direction Magazine
Debbie Taylor, Castelli Gallery
Andy Warhol and Fred Hughes

To Peter Palombi—good luck and good health

About the author

Brad Benedict is a cofounder of Paper Moon Graphics and is a partner in several Los Angeles boutiques: Heaven, Bijou, and Nickelodeon. He lectures at California State University at Northridge and coauthored, with Linda Barton, Phonographics: Contemporary Album Cover Art and Design (Macmillan 1977). Brad lives in Los Angeles.